Richmond upon Thames Libraries

Renew online at www.richmond.gov.uk/libraries

First published in Great Britain in 2021
by The Watts Publishing Group
© The Watts Publishing Group 2021

Managing editor: Victoria Brooker
Design: Paul Cherrill

ISBN: 978 1 4451 8144 8 (hbk)
ISBN: 978 1 4451 8145 5 (pbk)

Printed in Dubai

Franklin Watts
An imprint of Hachette Children's Group
Part of The Watts Publishing Group
Carmelite House
50 Victoria Embankment
London EC4Y 0DZ

An Hachette UK Company
www.hachette.co.uk
www.franklinwatts.co.uk

MIX
Paper from
responsible sources
FSC® C104740

Acknowledgements:

iSTOCK: Hadynyah 23c; highviews 9b; Noppasin 28-29 b; Powerofforever 18r;
Vectomart: cover flag; Vectomart front cover tc. Shutterstock: Allies Interactive
front cover tcr & cr; Andrey Armyagov 2,12-13; Valshak Babu front cover cl;
Bashbox 27tr; Glen Berlin 9c; BlackSTAR- Fotografie front cover ct; Catwalker 29t;
OlegD 17t; Viktar Dzerkach 6c; Amni G 25bl; Davide Gandolfi 6b,18b, 31;
Indian Food Images front cover bl, 9t; Anton Jankovoy 8b; Jayakumar 16b;
Filip Jedraszak 7c; Kamarulzmanganu 19cr; Mirko Kuzmanovic 27c; Hari Mahidhar 24b;
Don Mammoser front cover br, 17c; Manju Mandavya 5c; Matrix Images 5b;
Arun Sambhu Mishra 19l; Rudra Narayan Mitra front cover blr; Eo Naya 23b;
Niladrilovesphotography 12t; Nomad1988 8c; Oceloti front cover tbg, clb/g, cr b/g;
Snehal Jeevan Pailkar 15b; Olga Popova 28t; Paul Prescott 24t; Rahul Ramachandram
front cover tl; Reddees 15br; Jeremy Richards 4; Dmitry Rukhlenko front cover c;
Sumit Saraswat 19br; Sarunyu_foto 5t; Seb c'est bien 1,7b; Harshit Srivastava 26bc;
Aravind Teki front cover tcl; Tingling1 7t; TripDeeDee Photo 28bl;
Vectomart front cover tr & bc; VLADJ55 16t; Didier Wuthrich 17b; Danny Ye 26r.
Wikimedia Commons: Indian Institute of Science PD; Nesrad CC SA 4.0;
Washington Dept Education PD 27b; 30-32 MuchMania.

Every attempt has been made to clear copyright.
Should there be any inadvertent omission, please apply
to the publisher for rectification.

CONTENTS

Introducing India

Namaste! Welcome to India! Shaped roughly like a diamond, India has a land area of some 3,288,000 square kilometres. It is the largest country in South Asia, and the seventh biggest in the world. On land, India has borders with Bangladesh, Bhutan, Myanmar, China, Nepal and Pakistan. It has around 7,000 km of coastline, along the Bay of Bengal and the Arabian Sea (parts of the Indian Ocean).

Republic Of India

India became a republic on 26 January 1950. To mark this date, a grand parade is held each year in New Delhi, India's capital. India is also the world's largest democracy (a country whose government is directly elected by the people). In the 2019 general election, more than 600 million people voted. The president is head of state and the prime minister is head of the government. India is made up of 28 states and eight union territories.

INDIAN FLAG

The Indian flag has three equal, horizontal stripes in saffron (orange), white and green. In the centre of the white band is a dark-blue, 24-spoked wheel called a *chakra*. Each part of the flag has a special meaning. Saffron stands for strength and courage; white for peace and truth; and green for fertility and growth. The chakra wheel represents life and change.

The national anthem of India is 'Jana–Gana–Mana' which means 'You are the ruler of the minds of the people'. Its words and music were written by the poet, Rabindranath Tagore (1861–1941), who won the Nobel Prize for Literature in 1913.

NATIONAL SYMBOL

The chakra symbol comes from an ancient sculpture, known as the Lion Capital. The sculpture shows four lions, facing the four corners of the Earth, with chakras below them. It originally stood on top of a tall sandstone pillar. It was carved in the 3rd century BCE on the order of the Indian emperor, Ashoka. Today, it is the national symbol of India.

INDIAN LANGUAGES

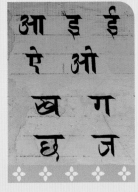

Namaste means 'hello' in Hindi, one of the many Indian languages. There are 22 other official languages, together with hundreds of local dialects. English is widely spoken. Different languages use different alphabets. Hindi is written in Devanagari. The letters in a word are joined by a line running across the top.

The official currency of India is the rupee. One rupee is divided into 100 paise. Large amounts of rupees are counted in hundreds of thousands, and given special names. A lakh is 100,000 rupees. A crore is 10,000,000 rupees (100 lakh).

When people say Namaste, they put their hands together.

Around India

India is a huge country, and its landscapes and climate vary enormously. There are ice-capped mountains, great rivers, sandy deserts, rolling plains, and tropical forests. The climate ranges from alpine and temperate in the north, to tropical in the south.

Sacred River

The River Ganges flows 2,525 km from the Himalayas, right across India to the Bay of Bengal. It is India's longest river and millions of people live along its banks. It is also a sacred river for Hindus, who believe that bathing in the water will wash away their bad deeds.

Mighty Mountains

The mighty Himalayas stretch across the north of India. This dramatic mountain range boasts nine out of ten of the highest mountains on Earth. One peak, Kanchenjunga, is 8,586 m tall. It is the highest mountain in India and the third highest in the world.

Monsoon Rains

Most of India has three seasons – a hot, dry spring; a hot, wet summer and a cool, dry winter. The climate is controlled by monsoon winds that change directions with the seasons. In the wet season, they bring heavy rains which farmers rely on for their crops.

Golden Temple

In the city of Amritsar stands the Golden Temple, the most sacred site for Sikhs. Designed in the 16th century, it is made from marble and covered in copper and gold. Its four doors symbolise that the Sikh religion is open to everyone.

Taj Mahal

The stunning Taj Mahal overlooks the River Yamuna in the city of Agra. It was built by the Mughal emperor, Shah Jahan, in memory of his wife, Mumtaz. Shah Jahan wanted it to be the most beautiful building ever seen and hired thousands of the best craftsmen from all over the world. Work began in 1632 and lasted for almost 20 years.

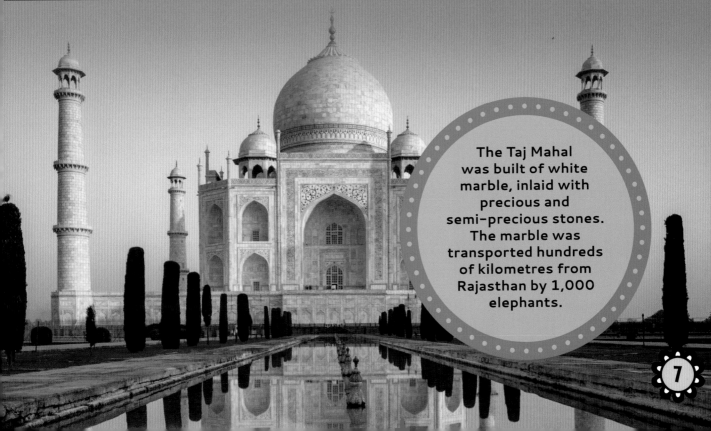

The Taj Mahal was built of white marble, inlaid with precious and semi-precious stones. The marble was transported hundreds of kilometres from Rajasthan by 1,000 elephants.

Indian Food

Food is very important in Indian culture and religion. It varies from place to place, depending on a region's climate, land and crops. Bread, such as chapattis and naans, are popular in the north, where wheat grows. More rice is grown and eaten in the south.

Farming and Crops

Around half of Indians work as farmers, or rely on agriculture for their living. Most farms are quite small and farmers are often poor. They cannot afford modern machinery and often use traditional methods, such as bullock ploughs, to prepare their fields. The main crops grown are rice (below), wheat, pulses and vegetables.

DID YOU KNOW?

Mangoes are India's national fruit. More mangoes are grown, and eaten, in India than anywhere else in the world. There are hundreds of different kinds.

Vegetarian Food

Three-quarters of Indians are Hindus, who follow the religion of Hinduism (see page 16). One of their most important beliefs is showing respect to all living things, which means not harming or killing them. Because of this, most Hindus are vegetarians. Some eat chicken, and fish, if they live along the coast, but they do not eat beef. They believe that cows are sacred animals because they produce milk, a vital source of nourishment.

Street Food

In every town and city in India, there are stalls selling food. This ranges from bags of puffed rice, to deep-fried pakoras, or plates of rice and dhal. Food is often washed down with hot, sweet, milky chai (tea), traditionally served in small, clay cups.

Sweet Tooth

Indian sweets (right) are very popular. Some are sticky and syrupy, such as *jalebi* and *gulab jamun*. Others, such as *rasgullas* and *sandesh*, are made from milk or curd cheese. Boxes of sweets are given as gifts on special occasions, such as weddings and festivals.

Vegetable Curry

Indian cooks like to flavour their dishes with spices, such as cumin, coriander, turmeric, fenugreek, cardamon, asafoetida and chilli. But be careful – too much chilli can make food eye-wateringly hot. This recipe will give you a very mild curry. It feeds two people and tastes good served with rice or chapattis. Ask an adult to help you make this.

1. Wash and peel two medium-sized potatoes and cut them into 2.5 cm cubes.

2. Partly fill the medium-sized saucepan with water. Put the pan on the ring and turn the heat to high. When the water boils, carefully add the potatoes and cook them for five minutes.

3. While the potatoes are cooking, chop a medium-sized cauliflower into small florets and throw away any thick stalks. When the potatoes are ready, drain the water away using a sieve.

4. Gently heat 5 tbsp oil in a large saucepan over a medium heat.

5. Mix 1/4 tsp chilli powder, 1/2 tsp cumin seeds, 1 tsp garam masala, 1 tsp salt and 1 tsp turmeric powder in a bowl.

6. Tip the spice mixture into the saucepan with the oil, add 2 heaped tsp tomato puree and stir.

Now add the potatoes and cauliflower and cook for about three minutes, stirring continuously.

7. Add 120 ml water to the saucepan, turn up the heat and bring the water to the boil.

9. Meanwhile, chop a handful of fresh coriander or parsley into tiny pieces.

8. Turn the heat down and leave your curry to simmer gently for about 15 minutes. Stir occasionally.

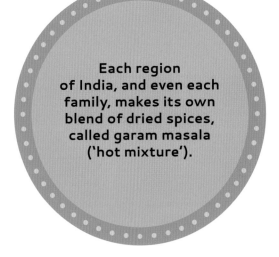

Each region of India, and even each family, makes its own blend of dried spices, called garam masala ('hot mixture').

10. When your curry is cooked, spoon it into the serving dish, sprinkle the chopped coriander or parsley on top, and serve it hot.

Life In India

More than 1.3 billion people live in India, more than in any other country apart from China. However, the population is still growing and may overtake China in the next ten years. Despite many people being very poor, Indian life is full of colour and bustle, a real mixture of modern and traditional.

City Living

Some people leave their family villages and travel to big cities, such as Mumbai (below), in search of work. They find jobs and send their wages back home, if they can. Indian cities are very crowded. Many poor people live in slums, without proper water supplies or sanitation. In contrast, rich city dwellers often live in luxury in large, modern blocks of flats.

VILLAGE INDIA

Around two-thirds of Indians live in thousands of villages, scattered all over India. Most villagers live in simple, one-storey houses. Wealthier people have larger houses, sometimes built around an open-air courtyard. A village may also have a well, a mandir or mosque, a few shops, a tea stall and a school.

FAMILIES

Traditionally, Indians lived in extended families, with children, parents, grandparents, uncles, aunts and cousins all under the same roof. When an Indian girl got married, she went to live with her husband's family. Many Indians still follow these customs, although some now choose to set up their own, separate homes.

SCHOOL DAYS

There are more than 1.5 million schools in India, with more than 8.5 million teachers. Indian children must go to school from the ages of 6 to 14. School is free for everyone and three-quarters of Indians can read and write. In poor areas, such as slums, however, classrooms are overcrowded and there are not enough books and other supplies to go around.

IN THE NEWS

Each year, around 17,000 newspapers are produced in India, in print and digital forms. Two of the most famous are the *Statesman* and the *Times of India*, both written in English. Around 200 million homes have television. India has around 600 million Internet users, and millions of people use social networks, such as Facebook and Twitter.

India has three of the world's biggest cities – New Delhi, Mumbai and Kolkata. More than 31 million people live in New Delhi.

PUTTING ON A SARI

YOU WILL NEED:
Short-sleeved T-shirt
Long petticoat
4 m length of material

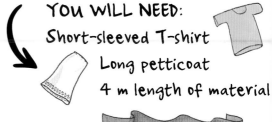

Many Indian women wear saris, made from long lengths of silk or cotton cloth. The cloth is wrapped around the waist and over the shoulder. It is worn over a petticoat and top. Putting on a sari takes practice. Here you can see what to do:

1. Put on the petticoat and T-shirt. Wrap one end of the material around your waist to form half a skirt and tuck the edge into the waistband of your petticoat.

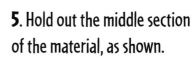

2. Pick up the other end of the material and pull it around the back of your waist ...

3. ... across your chest...

4. ... and up over your shoulder. The loose end of the material should drape down your back to your knees.

5. Hold out the middle section of the material, as shown.

6. Fold the loose material like a fan until the 'skirt' fits you. Tuck the tops of the folds into your petticoat's waistband. The folds should face the same way as the shoulder covered by the loose end of your sari.

7. Check that the hem at the bottom of your sari is even, and straighten the material draped over your shoulder.

SPORT AND LEISURE

People in India work hard, but also make the most of their free time. Playing and watching cricket, going to the cinema, flying kites and enjoying traditional music and dancing are popular ways of having fun.

CRICKET MAD

Cricket is the most popular sport in India, by a very long way! Everywhere you go, you see people playing cricket in the streets and on playing fields. The national team are closely followed and their performances, good and bad, are much discussed. Eden Gardens in Kolkata is one of the most famous stadiums in the world, with room for 70,000 fans.

BOLLYWOOD

India has the world's largest film industry. The 'Bollywood' studios in Mumbai make hundreds of Hindi-language films every year. Every day, millions of Indians go to the cinema to watch the latest blockbusters, starring superstar actors and actresses. Films are often packed with action, singing and dancing and can last for several hours.

INDIAN DANCE

Dating back hundreds of years, Kathakali is a traditional style of Indian dance from South India. Dancers perform stories from the Hindu epic poems. They wear elaborate costumes and masks, with brightly coloured make-up. Each detail, including colours, has a special meaning for the audience.

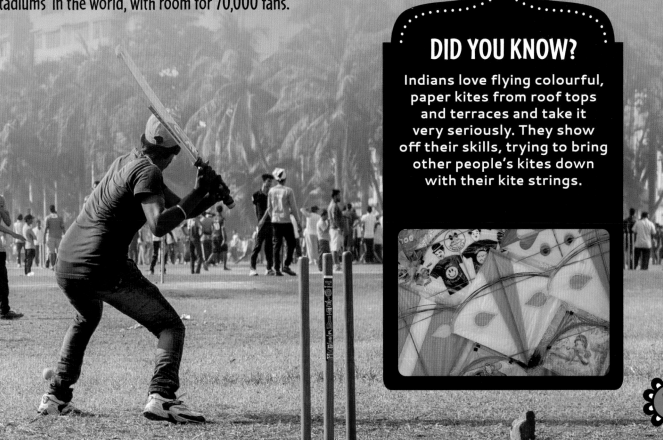

DID YOU KNOW?

Indians love flying colourful, paper kites from roof tops and terraces and take it very seriously. They show off their skills, trying to bring other people's kites down with their kite strings.

RELIGION IN INDIA

In India, religion is an essential part of everyday life and culture and many different faiths are followed. The main religion is Hinduism, but there are also millions of Muslims, Christians, Sikhs, Buddhists and Jains.

HINDU BELIEFS

About eight out of ten Indians are Hindus. Most believe in Brahman, a great spirit that exists beyond the material world. Some Hindus call Brahman 'God'. On Earth, Brahman is represented by hundreds of different gods and goddesses. Hindus also believe in reincarnation – when a person's soul is reborn in a different body when they die. What their next life is depends on how well or badly they have lived this one. This is called karma.

HINDU WORSHIP

Many Hindus visit the mandir (temple) to take part in *puja*, an Indian word meaning 'worship' or 'giving honour'. Each mandir is dedicated to a god, goddess or holy person and their sacred image stands in the main shrine. Hindus believe that Brahman is present in the sacred image. Many Hindus also have a small shrine, or shrine room, at home.

ISLAM

Millions of Indians are Muslims, who follow the religion of Islam. They believe in one God, called Allah, who sent messengers, called prophets, to teach people how to live a good life. The last and greatest prophet was Muhammad (pbuh). Muslims must pray at five set times a day, as instructed by Allah in the Holy Qur'an, their sacred book.

SIKH BELIEFS

The Sikh religion was begun in north-west India in 1499, by a holy man, called Guru Nanak. Sikhs worship in buildings, called gurdwaras, in front of the Guru Granth Sahib, their sacred book. Traditionally, they wear five signs of their faith, known as the Five Ks. These are: Kesh (uncut hair), Kangha (wooden comb), Kirpan (dagger), Kara (steel bangle) and Kachera (white undershorts).

CHRISTIANITY

After Hinduism and Islam, Christianity is India's third largest religion. Christianity was brought to India by Portuguese traders in the 16th century. They were Roman Catholics and many Indians still follow the Christian faith. In the states of Goa and Kerala, there are historic churches and monasteries, as well as new churches being built.

Festival Time

There is a festival almost every day, somewhere in India, and hundreds throughout the year. Some are local village celebrations; others involve the whole country. There are also national holidays, such as Republic Day on 26 January.

Festival of Light

In October or November, Hindus celebrate the festival of Divali. This marks the start of the New Year and is dedicated to Lakshmi, the goddess of wealth and good fortune. It is also the time when Hindus remember the story of the god, Rama, and his wife, Sita. People light little lamps to guide Rama and Sita home. They exchange cards and gifts of new clothes and jewellery and watch firework displays.

Spring Celebration

The festival of Holi is one of the happiest times of the Hindu year. It falls in February or March, and celebrates the beginning of spring. Traditionally, this was when farmers brought in the first wheat harvest of the year. Many stories are linked to Holi. The most famous tells of Prince Prahlad, who defeats Holika, a wicked witch. On the first night of Holi, people build bonfires and burn models of Holika.

DID YOU KNOW?

At Holi, people have fun drenching each other with coloured powders mixed with water. This remembers a story about the god, Krishna, who played the same trick on his friends.

Holy Month

During the month of Ramadan, Muslims fast (go without food and drink) from daybreak until sunset. Ramadan remembers the time when Allah sent down the first words of the Holy Qur'an. By fasting, Muslims show thanks to Allah and learn how to appreciate how lucky they are to have enough to eat and drink at other times.

Breaking The Fast

Muslims mark the end of Ramadan with the great festival of Id-ul-Fitr. It starts when the new moon appears in the night sky. People go to the mosque for prayers, then celebrate at home with their friends and families and a delicious Id feast. They also give a gift of money to charity – enough to provide a meal for someone in need.

Happy Birthday

Gurpurbs are Sikh festivals that remember key times in the lives of the ten Sikh Gurus (holy teachers), such as their birthdays and deaths. Sikhs celebrate Gurpurbs with prayers in the gurdwara and street processions. The Guru Granth Sahib, the Sikh holy book, is read from beginning to end. This takes about 48 hours, with a team of readers taking turns.

Putting On A Shadow Show

Behind many Indian festivals, there are stories of the gods and goddesses. The story of Divali tells of the god, Rama, and his wife, Sita. Banished from their homeland, they are forced to live in the forest. There, Sita is kidnapped by Ravana, an evil, 10-headed demon king. Helped by a huge army of monkeys and bears, Rama sets off to rescue her. He fights a fierce battle with Ravana, eventually killing him with a golden arrow. Rama and Sita return home in triumph, to be crowned king and queen.

Shadow Story

The story of Divali is told in books, TV series and plays. In South India, shadow puppet shows are put on in temples, in honour of the goddess, Bhadrakali. Legend says that she could not watch Rama's struggle with Ravana because she was fighting a battle of her own. So, a shadow version of events was created for her instead.

HOW TO STAGE YOUR OWN SHADOW SHOW

The wood measurements given here will make a shadow theatre 75 cm long and 32 cm high. You can, of course, make your shadow theatre and puppets any size you like as long as they are easy to see at a distance. Ask an adult to help you.

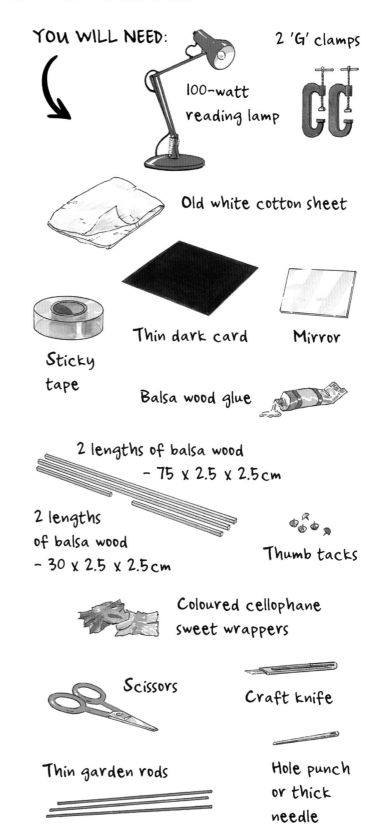

YOU WILL NEED:

100-watt reading lamp

2 'G' clamps

Old white cotton sheet

Sticky tape

Thin dark card

Mirror

Balsa wood glue

2 lengths of balsa wood – 75 x 2.5 x 2.5cm

2 lengths of balsa wood – 30 x 2.5 x 2.5cm

Thumb tacks

Coloured cellophane sweet wrappers

Scissors

Craft knife

Thin garden rods

Hole punch or thick needle

1. Glue the lengths of balsa wood together to make a frame.

2. Cut out a piece of sheet, big enough to cover one side of your frame. Gently stretch the material over the frame and pin it on opposite sides with the thumb tacks. Stretch the material again and pin the remaining sides.

3. Cover a high table with a tablecloth and fix your screen to it with the 'G' clamps. The tablecloth will hide your

body when you sit behind the screen. Your audience will sit on the other side of the screen to watch the play.

4. Ask an adult to help you set up the reading lamp behind your screen. The lamp should be higher than your head will be when you are sitting down, to stop your shadow from appearing on the screen.

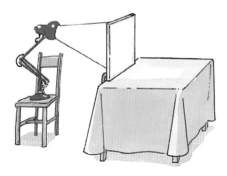

HOW TO MAKE THE SHADOW PUPPETS

1. Draw the outline of a puppet on the card and cut it out.

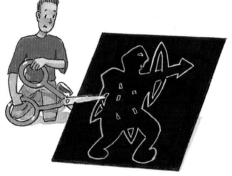

2. Using the hole punch or needle, make slits and holes in your puppet to suggest eyes, costume and jewellery. When the light shines on these holes, they will show through as white.

If you want to create colour effects, stick some coloured cellophane over the cuts.

3. Tape a garden rod to the back of your puppet with sticky tape so that you can move the puppet from below. Then make more puppets in the same way.

Some Indian shadow puppets are 2 m tall!

Stand a mirror in front of your screen as shown, and turn on the reading lamp. Now try pressing your puppets against the screen and then holding them further away. If you look in the mirror as you do this, you'll be able to see the different types of shadows you are making.

When you've seen what your puppets' shadows can do, invent a play for them. Cut out some card scenery and wedge it between the back of your screen and the frame. (Don't forget to remove the mirror when you stage your play in front of an audience.)

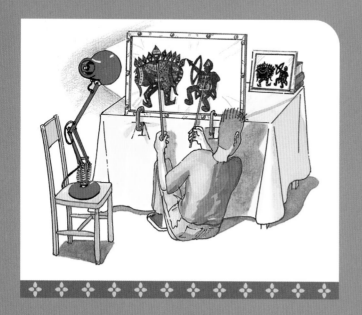

DID YOU KNOW?

The story of Rama and Sita comes from the Ramayana, one of the Hindu sacred texts. The Ramayana is a long poem of 24,000 verses, composed thousands of years ago.

ARTS AND CRAFTS

Traditional Indian arts and handicrafts are famous throughout the world. They include miniature paintings, brass work, ceramics, fabrics and fabric designs. Many goods are made by small, family-run businesses. Skills are passed down from one generation to the next.

FABULOUS FABRICS

India is one of the world's top producers of cotton and silk. Each region has its own traditional ways of dying and decorating cloth. In Varanasi, gold and silver thread are woven into super-fine silk. Saris made from this silk are often worn at weddings. A speciality of Gujarat and Rajasthan is mirror work. Tiny mirrors are sewn on to cotton cloth.

DID YOU KNOW?

Images of the Hindu gods and goddesses are often carved from sandalwood, which has a pleasant, spicy smell.

JEWELS OF INDIA

Highly skilled Indian jewellers produce beautiful jewellery from gold, silver and precious stones. Jewellery is very popular in India. Hindu women often wear lots of bangles. Traditionally, this shows that they are married, but bangles are also very fashionable. Extra-special jewellery is worn for weddings, such as ornate earrings, nose rings and head pieces.

GETTING ABOUT

It may seem that India is always on the move! People make long journeys by train, plane and bus to visit relatives, attend weddings and make pilgrimages to holy places. City streets are full of noise and traffic, as people travel to work and school by car, taxi and rickshaw. Traffic jams are very common, often caused by sacred cows wandering into the road.

INDIAN RAILWAYS

India has one of the largest railway networks in the world, with around 125,000 km of track and more than 7,000 stations. More than 20 million people travel by rail every day, and commuter trains, especially, get very crowded.

METRO LINES

India's first metro system opened in the city of Kolkata in 1984, using a mixture of underground and overground trains. The busiest metro is in Delhi. It has ten lines running to more than 250 stations all over the city.

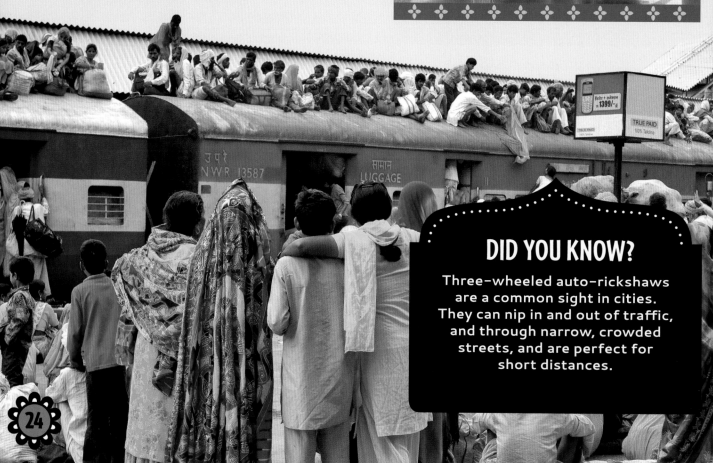

DID YOU KNOW?

Three-wheeled auto-rickshaws are a common sight in cities. They can nip in and out of traffic, and through narrow, crowded streets, and are perfect for short distances.

Hi-Tech India

In recent years, India has become a world leader in science and technology. Its technology companies produce cutting-edge software and its space programme has launched satellites and sent missions to the Moon.

Digital Hub

Many young Indians study science, technology or engineering. They may then go to work for one of India's up-and-coming tech companies, such as Infosys in Bangalore (below). The city of Bangalore in southern India is the centre for digital technology, nuclear science, space sciences and computing. More than 1.5 million people work for IT companies in Bangalore.

Space Race

In September 2014, India made history when its Mars Orbiter Mission successfully entered Mars' orbit. This was a huge achievement for the country's space scientists. It was India's first mission to another planet and made India the first Asian country to reach Mars. A few years earlier, India launched its Moon Impact Probe. The probe landed on the Moon on 14 November 2008 and discovered evidence of water.

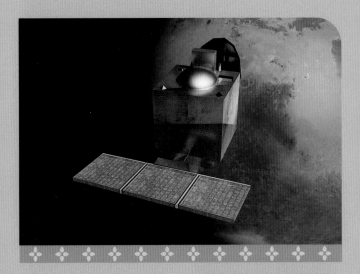

India Innovation

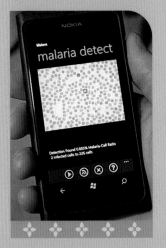

Malaria is a disease that kills millions of people in India and around the world. In 2014, scientists at the Indian Institute of Science converted a smartphone into a device that could detect malaria quickly and easily, without the need for lots of blood tests. They replaced the phone's camera with a microscope which can detect malaria in a tiny drop of blood.

History of India

India is an ancient country. Over the centuries, its land and riches have attracted settlers and explorers, many of whom stayed on as rulers. Each left its mark on the country, through its culture, religion and architecture. Here are just some of the many highlights from India's long and colourful history.

Indus Valley

The first great civilisation in India grew up along the banks of the Indus river (today in Pakistan) in around 3000 BCE. By 2500 BCE, it had reached the height of its power. Its centres were the cities of Harappa and Mohenjo Daro, laid out along careful plans. Houses were built of mud bricks and had bathrooms and sophisticated drainage systems. Each city had a religious centre and huge granaries for storing precious supplies of grain.

Emperor Ashoka

In 269 BCE, Ashoka Maurya came to the throne and ruled over most of India. In 260 BCE, Ashoka fought a successful but bloody war, which left tens of thousands of people dead.

Filled with remorse, Ashoka became a Buddhist and followed the Buddha's teachings on peace and non-violence. He had these teachings carved on cave walls and rocks (above) around his empire for everyone to read. Ashoka was keen to hear ordinary people's opinions and travelled widely through his empire. He tried to make people's lives easier by building roads and rest houses and setting up free hospitals.

GUPTA GLORY

Around 320 CE, another great empire rose in India – the Guptas. Under the Gupta kings, Hinduism became India's main religion and literature, art, architecture and science flourished. Many temples and colleges were built. Trade in textiles, such as cotton, silk, and linen, made the empire rich.

MUGHAL EMPIRE

During the 16th century, India was conquered by Muslims from the north west. They were called the Mughals. For two hundred years, they ruled a mighty empire, famous for its fine paintings, beautiful buildings and splendid gardens. The greatest Mughal emperor was Akbar, who ruled for 49 years. He had a deep interest in reading and religion and employed many non-Muslims at his court.

THE GREAT MUGHALS
Babur – reigned 1526–1530
Humayun – reigned 1530–1540; 1555–1556
Akbar – reigned 1556–1605
Jahangir – reigned 1605–1627
Shah Jahan – reigned 1627–1658
Aurangzeb – reigned 1658–1707

British Raj

By 1756, Mughal power was at an end and the British were set to take control of India. They had come to India for trade but had gradually strengthened their power and position. In 1876, Queen Victoria was proclaimed Empress of India. India remained part of the British Empire until it won independence in 1947.

Indian Independence

At the end of the 19th century, a group of young, educated Indians formed a political party, called the Indian National Congress. Its aim was to campaign for a greater say for Indians in how they ran their country. The British agreed to many of their requests, but also broke many promises. The 'Quit India' movement grew stronger after the Second World War and, on 14 August 1947, India won its freedom. In the Indian Parliament, the new prime minister, Jawaharlal Nehru (right), gave an historic speech about India's destiny being fulfilled.

Mahatma Gandhi

One of the most important campaigners for independence was Mohandas Gandhi (1869–1948). He later became known as 'Mahatma' which means 'Great Soul'. After studying law in England, Gandhi (right) took a job in South Africa. In 1915, he returned to India to join the freedom struggle. Gandhi believed in non-violent resistance. He encouraged Indians to protest against British rule, but not to use violence, even if they were attacked.

Since Independence

After independence, India began taking steps to become a modern nation. There were advances in farming, industry and communication. Since then, India has progressed to become one of the world's leading economies. There are still many problems – millions of people live in great poverty – but India today is a fascinating mix of traditional and modern, such as Bangalore (below), with sights and sounds to dazzle your senses.

गांधी शताब्दी

GANDHI CENTENARY

पै. प.
75

1869–1969

भारत INDIA

In the years leading to independence, tension grew between Hindus and Muslims. The British decided to divide the country into two – mainly Hindu India and mainly Muslim Pakistan. This became known as 'Partition'. In the chaos and violence that followed, millions of people were forced to leave their homes, and more than 500,000 were killed.

GLOSSARY

alpine a high mountain, climate or habitat

civilisation a society which is very advanced in science, technology, the arts, government and law

democracy a country that is governed by ministers, elected by the people of the country

dialect a different way of speaking a language, with its own pronunciation and phrases

epic poem a long poem that tell the story of the lives and actions of gods and heroes

extended family a family which includes parents, children, grandparents and other relatives

granary a building where grain is stored.

gurdwara a places where Sikhs go to meet and worship

independence becoming free from another country's rule

malaria a deadly tropical disease spread by mosquitoes

mandir a place where Hindus go to meet and worship

monsoon a seasonal change of weather that brings heavy rainfall and a change in wind direction

mosque a place where Muslims go to meet and worship

Muslim a follower of the religion of Islam

non-violence not using violence, even if someone is being violent towards you

pulse a seed eaten as food, such as lentils, chickpeas and beans

republic a country which has a president as its head of state

sacred something that is important or special to a religion

sandalwood a type of wood that has a pleasant, spicy smell

shrine a sacred place where people can pray. It may be part of another room or building.

slums very poor, overcrowded areas in a city

state one of the areas of India with its own state government

temperate a climate that has mild temperatures

union territory areas of India that don't have their own governments but are ruled by the central government

vegetarian someone who doesn't eat meat

FIND OUT MORE

BOOKS

Blue Worlds: The Indian Ocean
Anita Ganeri (Franklin Watts, 2022)

Expedition Diaries: Indian Lowlands
Simon Chapman (Franklin Watts, 2022)

Lonely Planet India (Travel Guide)
Joe Bindloss and others (Lonely Planet, 2022)

Journey through India
Anita Ganeri (Franklin Watts, 2016)

WEBSITES

www.kids.nationalgeographic.com/geography/countries/article/india
This National Geographic webpage gives a quick introduction to India,
with fast facts and stunning photos.

www.lonelyplanet.com/india
Lonely Planet gives you lots of historical and geographical information,
as well as tips for the best places to visit in India.

INDEX